T0158846

ROBERT E. SLAVIN

Damp Yankees
(Another American Gobsmacked by England)

iUniverse, Inc.

Bloomington

Damp Yankees
(Another American Gobsmacked by England)

Copyright © 2011 Robert E. Slavin

All rights reserved. No part of this book may be used or reproduced by any means, graphic, electronic, or mechanical, including photocopying, recording, taping or by any information storage retrieval system without the written permission of the publisher except in the case of brief quotations embodied in critical articles and reviews.

iUniverse books may be ordered through booksellers or by contacting:

iUniverse
1663 Liberty Drive
Bloomington, IN 47403
www.iuniverse.com
1-800-Authors (1-800-288-4677)

Because of the dynamic nature of the Internet, any Web addresses or links contained in this book may have changed since publication and may no longer be valid. The views expressed in this work are solely those of the author and do not necessarily reflect the views of the publisher, and the publisher hereby disclaims any responsibility for them.

Any people depicted in stock imagery provided by Thinkstock are models, and such images are being used for illustrative purposes only.

Certain stock imagery © Thinkstock.

ISBN: 978-1-4620-4085-8 (sc)
ISBN: 978-1-4620-4086-5 (e)

Printed in the United States of America

iUniverse rev. date: 8/9/2011

Foreword

by Charles Dickens

It is the best of books, it is the worst of books; too brief to be a novel, too novel to be a picaresque, too picaresque to be a brief. There is much in this slim volume that is wise and true, but alas, that which is wise is not true and that which is true is not wise. Droll it may be, even risible at times, but these pages carry a thorn among the daffodils. Has great England sunk to such a low estate as to be an object of jest for mere Americans?

C. D.
Westminster Abbey

Preface

It was the dark days of 2006. There I was, minding my own business, when I got into a bit of a tiff with the Bush administration. As a result, I found myself exiled from Baltimore to York, the loveliest medieval city in England. Imagine a twist on Genesis: Adam and Eve are banished to Eden after having an argument with the snake. Not bad. And while I'm wandering the crooked snickelways of York and the moors and dales around Yorkshire, the snake had to retire to Texas and pretend to like pork rinds.

So what is it like to be an American in England? This book is my answer. My experience is, of course, colored by where I'm from and where I live in England. Baltimore is in the most England-like part of the United States, the part that lies within fifty miles of the DC-to-Boston Amtrak line. I'm sure that England would look very different to someone from Texas or Montana. Although my work takes me to London frequently, I live in the North, a very, very different place from the England experienced by most Americans.

Disclaimer:

I am not a trained journalist, so any observations reported in this book may be true.

Another disclaimer:

"England" is a completely fictitious location. Any resemblance to any actual country, such as Italy, is coincidental.

Editor's note:

Enough with the disclaimers already! Get on with the England!

Contents

DAMP YANKEES

The most important thing to say about the English and the Americans is that they are crazy about one another. Americans think of English people as slightly smarter Americans. The English think of Americans as slightly sexier English people. Hearing an English accent, Americans break into smiles. Millions of Americans got up at four in the morning to watch the royal wedding. I think Jamaicans and Trinidadians are especially popular in the United States because of their English accents. On a car trip from San Francisco to Oregon, I once picked up a hitchhiker who turned out to be English. He complained bitterly that wherever he went Americans loved him, fed him, put him up overnight. He wanted to sleep rough out on the frontier, but Americans were just too friendly. We approached my house in Portland at night, and I sheepishly offered him a bed and some food. He thanked me, but asked me to drop him in a city park to sleep outside.

I was surprised and delighted to find that especially outside of London, English people are equally enchanted by an American accent. I think we have much the same exotic-but-safe allure that the English have for us. In the abstract, we all have our national prejudices, and every once in a while, like when BP pollutes the entire Gulf of Mexico, the press plays up US/UK animosities. But up close and personal, people in our two nations like one another a lot more than we seem to like our own compatriots.

Americans who visit England invariably love absolutely everything about it, except the food, the warm beer, the cold rain, the swarms of American tourists, and the shocking prices. English people who visit the United States invariably love absolutely everything about it except the large portions served in American restaurants. What's odd about this is that while the things Americans complain about in England are exactly what the English themselves dislike about England. I've never heard an American complain about large portions. Here's a conversation you'll never hear: "I'm not going to that restaurant again. The food was wonderful, but the portions? Much too large. And the prices were low, too."

Geologists have found that rock formations in the eastern part of the United States are physically and chemically identical to those in Britain. So it is with our peoples. Americans (including me) may have no family connection whatsoever with Britain, but they still feel a strong tie to the place. When Americans read about the Spanish Armada, they root for the English. We fought the bloody redcoats in the American Revolution and the War of 1812, but we still root for the English at Waterloo, and if the United States can't win the World Cup, we root for England. Be they Eastern European, African American, Mediterranean, or Asian in origin, Americans think of English literary, cultural, and scientific accomplishments as their own. We think Shakespeare and Dickens and Gilbert and Sullivan and Conan Doyle and Darwin and Newton were really proto-Americans, and do not see them as foreign. Irish Americans try to resist the Anglophilia that comes with their US passport, but it's hard even for them.

THE VERY BEST THING ABOUT ENGLAND

To me, the very best thing about England is the love the English have for their land and its history. Outside of the London area and Stratford, the vast majority of visitors to any historical site in England are English, and every ruined castle or abbey, ancient garden, church, or museum, is kept in pristine condition and visited enthusiastically. I once visited the Holy Island of Lindisfarne on a cold, windswept day. Stinging pellets of rain were battering everything in sight. The island is linked by a low causeway to the mainland that is flooded at high tide. Driven by the wind, water was lapping inches away from the causeway. Who, I wondered, could possibly be visiting this desolate place on such a day?

When we got to the island, however, there were more than one hundred cars in a parking lot. A bus appeared, and people emerged from their cars. Cheerful, curious, eager English people wearing sensible clothing. The bus dropped us at Lindisfarne Castle, where a rain-delayed wedding caused the castle to close for a half hour. The visitors huddled for warmth in Quonset huts near the entrance, waited patiently, and finally went into the castle after the sodden (but happy) wedding party left. Throughout the day, swarms of tourists waded through ankle-high water to visit the wonderful exhibits and ruins of ancient religious communities.

Because of the enormous interest in every aspect of their history, the smallest and least significant of historical sites are lovingly tended. In East Yorkshire, Wharram Percy is an abandoned medieval village, currently consisting of grass-covered humps. Yet it is carefully kept up by a wonderful organization called English Heritage and frequently visited.

In a country with thousands of *standing* villages with twelfth century churches, it's not clear why anyone is interested in an abandoned village, but there it is, a well-marked historical sight with a parking lot with a placard showing a picture of the humps and text explaining the (utter lack of) history.

In a land not invaded since 1066, there is an awful lot of history still standing, and keeping it standing requires vast expenditures. If it hadn't been for the English Civil War in the 1600s, England would go bankrupt just keeping up all its castles. If Henry VIII hadn't wrecked hundreds of abbeys in the 1500s, England would be getting bailouts from the Greeks to keep everything in good condition.

The English also show their love of their land by walking all over it. More than five hundred organized rambling clubs have day hikes of ten miles or more and overnight hikes that can go for weeks, not to mention thousands of hikers who go on their own.

In a country that pays little attention to organized religion, Sunday rambles have become a sort of church of nature. Rambling groups have their own clergy, consisting of leaders who are required to hike a given route during the week before the ramble. One leader guides the faithful while another brings up the rear, nipping at the laggards' heels, to ensure that the whole flock is properly accounted for. Because even the smallest English towns are very concentrated, most of densely populated England is open land with great natural beauty.

The English passion for their land means that they tend their entire nation like a giant garden. You never see the trash, billboards, urban sprawl, or commercialization common in America. England has its grim urban neighborhoods and industrial blight, but there is hardly an Englishman outside of London who is not within ten miles of lovely scenery, fascinating history, and pleasures of the soul.

THE ENGLISH POPULATION: KEEPING IT UP

English children are delightful, and everyone loves them. The problem is that there aren't enough of them. I have a theory about why this is so.

I happen to live near Micklegate, the ancient road leading into the walled city of York. Micklegate is lined with bars and nightclubs. Every weekend night, there are flocks of young women cruising up and down Micklegate wearing matching clothing, and not much of it. They are dressed as cowgirls, bunnies, and hookers; you name it. Most of them are in hen parties or other female-bonding rituals. They come by the busload regardless of the weather; even in the dreadful blizzard of 2009–2010, there were bare-armed, barelegged young women without coats.[1] There are some men in Micklegate, but they are usually paired up with normally dressed girlfriends. The members of the hen parties seem to think they're supposed to be having a lot more fun than they are, but perhaps I'm not seeing them late enough in the evening.

But where are the men? Just before young men get married, their male friends throw them a stag party. This often involves cheap flights to somewhere in Eastern Europe known for cheap beer. The entire purpose, or so I've heard, is to get the groom-to-be completely drunk, get him into some embarrassing situation, and take pictures of him. England's young men start off the serious responsibilities of married life shortly after waking up chained to a railing in Bratislava wearing a pink jock strap and women's underwear on their head, with photos to prove it on Facebook. So here's a biological fact. If you keep your young men in Bratislava and your young women in Micklegate, you're not

---

1   I thought only Americans had the right to bare arms.

going to produce many cute English babies. Further, the popularity of marriage itself is plummeting. Perhaps the more sensible young men, the very ones who'd make the best dads, would rather not wake up nearly naked in Bratislava.

My proposed solution to England's baby crisis is to create incentives for young men to have their stag parties in the UK. A steep barf tax on discount airlines to Eastern Europe would do the trick. This would also greatly improve Britain's image in the world and would solve a serious balance-of-payments problem with Slovakia.

WOMEN

If you walk down the high street of any town in England, you'll see lovely, attractively dressed, sweet-tempered women. Goddesses, really. Of course, they're Polish. But English women are very nice too.

TRADITION

On a bridge over the upper Thames stands a surly adolescent wearing a Megadeth T-shirt. Ever so slowly, he collects a toll of twenty pence from every car, causing a huge backup every morning and afternoon. The bridge, in a town called Whitchurch, links Oxfordshire and Berkshire, so he is standing in the center of England's Silicon Valley. The people fuming in their expensive cars are England's creative, entrepreneurial elite, the very key to Britain's future, at least according to themselves. Yet every morning, a young twit in slow motion costs them fifteen minutes (and twenty pence) on their way to work.

The reason there is a toll on this particular bridge is that centuries ago, some family was given hereditary rights to charge this toll. I'm assuming that the nearly catatonic teenager is a descendant of this family, just on the basis that if he weren't, he'd have been sacked for his poor taste in music and general worldview.

Every high-tech tycoon waiting to cross this bridge would happily contribute whatever it took to buy out the family's toll rights. Yet the toll and the teenager remain, and will probably always remain, another bit of sand in the gears of progress.

One of the most endearing aspects of England is the deep respect for the past, the continuation of traditions just because they are traditions. Usually this love of tradition is charming, leading to all the pomp and fuss around the royals, the parliament, and much more. I once gave a speech at a primary school in Nottingham, after which the school cafeteria served lunch. Standing behind me in the queue was a man in elaborate robes and a gold chain, who turned out to be the actual sheriff of Nottingham. He now serves no particular function, he told me, but isn't that the whole point?

Yet the idea that tradition trumps everything also has maddening costs. Family-owned toll bridges are just the beginning. Next to the University of York is a twenty-five-acre common, called a stray in Yorkshire, on which cows and horses graze. The stray is just outside the walls of the old city, but well within the center of the modern city. It (and many others) exists because, hundreds of years ago, they were set aside to enable local people to graze their stock on land open to all. It's nice to see green space and cows in the middle of York, but this is a shocking use of space. Boston Common and other commons in New England, established for the same reasons, have long since become lovely urban parks. Yet the strays are not parks, and kids don't play in them because of the cows. The only reason for the strays to exist is, of course, is that they always have.

Getting anything done in England, especially with respect to land, is nearly impossible. Historical preservation is a huge issue, because in a nation so rich in history, every square foot of dirt has some history that may be worth preserving. But this is not the main problem. English traditions regarding land ownership are unbelievably arcane and complex.

I have a friend who owns a section of the Dart River in Devon, but he does not own the fishing rights, which are hugely expensive. If he wants to fish, he has to ask permission from the owners of the fishing rights, and if they want to fish, they have to ask him. One person may own even modern apartments but another may own the land. Some land cannot be bought or sold but only leased for ninety-nine years, and the land progressively loses value as the ninety-nine-year date approaches.

Every English person knows that the Whitchurch teenager must go, that the strays should be made into parks, and that land ownership should be made rational. Yet these things will probably never happen. Tradition has its bright trappings, but sometimes it ends up blocking the bridge to the future.

Honours

A colleague of mine was recently knighted. He described to me all the pomp and ceremony involved. A Royal Air Force officer instructed him exactly where he should stand and how close he was allowed to approach the queen (the issues of air and space between queen and knight must explain why the RAF serves this function). All this is exactly what Americans imagine—the English do pomp really well.

However, in the very same ceremony, a milkman from Melton Mowbray was awarded an MBE.[2] The milkman, who had performed valuable services over the years in reporting suspicious activities he saw on his rounds, appeared for his award costumed as a Friesian cow. He'd sewn big white cow-like patches on his black suit. He originally had a tail, he told the press, but his dog tore it off on his way out the door.

The queen, who has seen much worse, chatted amicably with the milkman and carried on with the ceremony. A spokesperson for the queen later suggested, however, that more solemn and appropriate attire might have been in order.

The juxtaposition of my friend knighted with a sword and an RAF escort, and a Leicestershire milkman dressed as a cow to meet the queen, sums up the silly seriousness and the serious silliness of the honours system in the UK. The English are deeply honored by honours, and my ordinarily modest and self-effacing friend will not stop people from calling him Sir John for the rest of his life. He fully appreciates the inherent humor in having a twenty-first-century science educator kneeling to be whacked on the shoulder with a sword. But it is also

---

2   Member of the British Empire.

deeply moving, just because English monarchs have been knighting knights since King Arthur was a pup, and now he's one of them. He doesn't get any castles or serfs, of course, and his kids will have to earn their own knighthoods, but there's something to be said for a system that makes it possible for a humble milkman to earn an MBE by helping out his neighbors, for a distinguished science educator to become a knight, and for both of them to be able to mock the whole system without fear of encountering the sharp end of the queen's sword. *Honi soit qui mal y pense.*[3]

---

3   "Shame on him who thinks ill of it." Motto of the Order of the Garter. How
      weird is that?

SPORTS

I was once walking in my neighborhood in Baltimore and came upon a cricket game played with great pleasure and enthusiasm by what appeared to be East Indian college students. There were girls as well as boys playing in ordinary clothing, and no one was keeping score, as far as I could tell.[4]

In four years in England, I've never seen anything comparable. I have seen young men dressed in white and playing formal cricket games, but never pick-up games like those common among Americans playing baseball, touch football, soccer, or basketball. American kids play baseball with whomever they can find, with any number of players on each side, and "ghost runners" to occupy bases if the runner's turn to bat comes up. On a trip to New Zealand, I saw kids everywhere playing informal games of rugby, just for fun. I sometimes see kids in England playing pick-up soccer games with a pair of coats at each end of the field to mark the goals as would be common in the United States, but most often if I get up close, I hear them yelling to one another in Italian or Spanish.

If my observation is correct, this might have a lot to do with the constant disappointment the English feel about their sports teams. They invented cricket, soccer, rugby, tennis, squash, and badminton, yet they rarely win at their own games. It may be that the players who love these games in other countries have thousands more hours of practice as kids before they begin to play competitively. South American kids,

---

4   Americans pride themselves on not understanding cricket, and as a proud
    American, I haven't a clue what they were really doing.

for example, rarely spend a whole hour without their feet contacting a soccer ball, even during weddings and funerals, including their own.

On the other hand, it may be that losing at sports is just part of the English psyche. It's a big world, and England often ranks quite well, but if the English team does not win outright, the whole country goes into a deep funk of depression. Moaning about the Ashes (cricket), or the Olympics, or the World Cup, or the America's Cup, or Wimbledon, may perversely be what binds England together. Since England plays as England, never the UK, sports is the one arena in which their inner Englishness can be given free rein, and the very essence of inner Englishness is a glum resignation to plod forward toward certain disappointment. If the English ever won the World Cup, for example, they'd be delighted, but a week later, they'd already be moaning in advance about the Ashes. In the recent World Cup, English fans were in a frenzy of excitement until England lost in a damp squib of a game with Germany. But at a certain level, I think many may have been secretly relieved. England is so good at moaning about sports, and everyone likes to do what they're best at.

NAMES

Britain has thirty thousand distinct names of towns, and somehow they keep them all straight. So why does each nation in the UK only have so few given names? Just about every Englishman (at least in my generation) is named Michael or Peter or James or John or Richard. Every Welshman is named David or Dylan. Scotsmen are all Ian or Robert. I don't know what happens in large Welsh families. They must have a David, a Dylan, a David II, a Dylan II, and so on. Names never used in America, like Nigel and Trevor and Alistair, must have been invented for third and fourth sons, when all the standard names have been used up. Women's names are equally scarce. English women of my age are usually Elizabeth, Susan, Margaret, or Anne, plus Mary for women of Irish origin. There is more faddism with girls' names, with loads of Dianas a few years ago for obvious reasons. (For equally obvious reasons, the name "Charles" fell entirely out of use.)

The problem with this lack of name diversity, of course, is that it causes a lot of mix-ups. If you greet your friend Michael or David across a crowded room, twelve heads swivel around. Boys write love letters to Elizabeth only to find out in horror that the wrong Elizabeth got the note. Girls spread malicious gossip about Anne and the wrong Anne is damaged. I think popular names should be rationed somehow. After a certain number of Peters in a given town, for example, the parents might be asked to choose a less common name, such as Bertram or Colin or Llewelyn. This would strike a blow for individuality, clarity, and good sense.

LONDON AND NON-LONDON

J ust about every American with a passport has been to London, and they all love it. For a huge city, it is marvelously livable with few tall buildings, lots of parks and green space, low crime, and lots to do.

To the English, however, London is something else. It plays a central role in everything of importance. The United States has separate centers for government, finance, business, moviemaking, and culture, but London fulfills all these functions. If you count nearby Oxford and Cambridge, in addition to the many top London universities, it is the center of academia as well. Because of London's primacy in every arena, every middle-class Englishman has two hometowns: his own and London.

Londoners are not arrogant about their preeminent status, but whenever someone from anywhere else has to meet with someone from London, the non-Londoner travels to London; it's rarely the reverse. The rationale, perhaps, is that the non-Londoner has or can find other things to do before or after a meeting, while there is little chance that the Londoner will find something else to do after a meeting in Bristol or Manchester or Sheffield. But there's also an attitude. Londoners think London is the kangaroo, the rest of England the joey. London is the Elephant and Castle, the rest of England is the man who follows with a shovel. Northerners, especially, resent this like heck, but since when have their opinions mattered?

To me, what is distinctively England is its glorious, especially medieval past. London has the Tower, Westminster Abbey, and the Houses of Parliament, which are fabulous, but the rest is Victorian to modern. What makes England England is its castles, churches, abbeys, ancient and picturesque towns, and gardens. Non-London is where England is truly England. London *has* museums, some of the finest in the world. Non-London *is* a museum. May it always be so.

Dam the English

One amazing thing about England is the flooding. In York, anyway, the Ouse River floods four or five times every winter. A famous pub on the river, in operation since the 1770s, floods every time. It has wooden tables in front, which are chained to the stone quay. When the Ouse floods, the tables float up a bit, but life otherwise goes on. Parking garages fill up with water, but most parkers get warnings to move their cars when a flood is coming.

If any American city flooded this often, the Army Corps of Engineers would be on it like a duck on a June bug. They'd be building dams and sluices and weirs and what all, solving the flood problem, creating hydroelectric power, and forming a recreational lake. They'd put in a fish ladder so the salmon could go back to Scotland, or wherever they go. All this construction would create thousands of jobs and loads of possibility for graft and corruption. In England, however, none of this happens. Instead, the English response to flooding is the same as their response to other weather-related problems: get wet.

KEEP ENGLAND GREEN—AND BLACK AND BLUE

E ngland has two great passions: energy conservation, and health and safety. The problem is they conflict.

In the interests of energy conservation, plus saving money, England has very little lighting in the evening. This in a country that gets dark at 3:00 half the year, and is overcast and drizzling to boot. This means that people are stumbling around in the dark all winter even before they start drinking.

In York, the university where I work is separated from part of the city by a stray, or common, where, according to some medieval statute, cows get to roam free at all times. There is a paved path through the stray, but not the least glimmer of a light. Anyone who walks or bikes home in the evening runs a major risk of life and limb. The bikers, who fly by at great speed, can hit the walkers. The walkers also risk stepping in cow poop, falling down, and then being run over by the bikes. The bikes risk running into the walkers, but even more, they risk running into the cows. This startles the cows and bruises the bikers.

Because the crime rate in York is so low, it does not occur to anyone that having students wandering through a pitch-black stray is problematic for any reason other than collisions. If anyone ever puts in lights, it will be to protect the cows (animal protection is another British passion).

It's not just the stray that's dark, of course. The whole country is dark. Perhaps one of the reasons for the low crime rate is that criminals can't find their victims half the year. Blackouts may have been a good idea in World War II, but enough already. It's time for England to lighten up.

WEATHER: RAINY, WITH A CHANCE OF RAIN

Well, I put it off as long as I could, but it's time to take on the touchiest topic of all between our countries. No, it's not David Beckham. It's the weather.

Americans universally believe that the weather in England is dreadful. English people completely agree, but they don't like to hear about it from Americans. The English think American weather is much better than theirs is, because when they go to the United States they go to Florida, which boasts sunny days and a Frenchman-free Disney World.

The problem is, most actual Americans do not live in Florida, for good reason. Florida is tacky beyond human imagining. It makes Blackpool look like a cathedral. The Florida Tackiness Council requires that Florida constantly maintain and upgrade its tackiness, because otherwise, everyone would move there and overwhelm their precious, limited reserves of coconut-scented suntan oil. California, which had to disband its own Tackiness Council due to Proposition 13, has grown explosively as a result, and has had to elect washed-up movie actors as governors to get people to move away.

Where most Americans really live, the weather is worse than England's. I was in York for the ferocious blizzard of 2009–2010. More than six inches of snow fell, and it did not immediately melt! Americans in the half of America north of Maryland have a word for weather like that: April. Even Atlanta, Georgia, gets more snow than London does. England doesn't even get that much rain. Its problem is that it's always overcast, and there is hardly any day in England when it couldn't rain. Also, when an Englishman can't stand it any more, he can put his family on a cheap flight to Spain or Portugal, where two hours later they're in a sunny, historic, interesting place with good beaches. When most Americans do the same, they have to go to, well … Florida. Not a pretty picture.

Gentle, frequent rain makes England green and clean, with a just-scrubbed feeling to its air. English rain is just the right backdrop for English castles and churches and other medieval remnants. All the great scientific and cultural creations of the English mind took place because their creators were stuck inside on rainy days with nothing else to do. The very empire owed its existence to Englishmen willing to risk everything in a quest for decent weather and interesting food. And the best thing about the rain is that it feels so good when it stops. There's no one happier than an Englishman is on a rare sunny day.

FOOD

To get an idea where English food got its awful reputation, start with the "full English breakfast,"[5] served in just about every hotel and restaurant in the country. It invariably includes a fried egg, a salty slice of ham, and two sausages so full of filler that they should be labeled "very few pigs were harmed in the creation of this sausage." There's always a broiled tomato (or possibly tomato glop), baked beans, a horrible deep-fried square of mashed potatoes, usually mushrooms, and quite often the most repulsive thing in English cookery: black pudding, a sort of blood sausage that tastes exactly as bad as it looks.

As you can see, the theme here is quantity and cholesterol. The full English breakfast, like much of traditional English food, is basically American comfort food. If you leave the black pudding alone, it has a certain heart-stopping hardiness. On Sundays, most pubs offer a Sunday carvery consisting of thin slices of beef swimming in gravy, buried in potatoes, cabbage, rutabagas, and a Yorkshire pudding, served with excellent beer. Filling, tasty, nothing fancy, but not nearly as bad as its reputation.

Best of all, you don't have to eat this stuff. Even the smallest town has at least one excellent Indian restaurant. Indian food provides a walk on the wild side for the English palate. Chinese, Thai, Italian, Spanish, and other ethnic restaurants are widely distributed and many outstanding English restaurants make innovative uses of local ingredients. If you're traveling, you are probably stuck with a full English breakfast, but after that, the offerings are diverse and excellent.

---

5   Known as the full Scottish breakfast in Scotland, the full Welsh breakfast in Wales, and the full Irish breakfast in Ireland, without the slightest difference or irony.

If you're cooking for yourself, it's possible to find most ingredients you could find in the United States, with terrific lamb, salmon, and local vegetables at reasonable prices. Most amazing, however, are the eggs. Grocery stores all have an astonishing variety, going from cheap eggs from "caged hens," to eggs from hens allowed to run and play in the forest. There are eggs from hens encouraged to pursue advanced university degrees, strolling down shady lanes discussing Sartre or Schopenhauer. The loving descriptions of the lives led by high-end hens must be galling to Englishmen whose standard of living is less than that of their eggs. The lovely gesture toward animal rights is touching, except that the eggs are sold right next to the meat counter displaying the remains of less fortunate lambs, pigs, steers, and not to put too fine a point on it, hens, perhaps those who failed their university admissions exams.

MONEY

The English are rather funny about money. They don't like to spend it, but they also don't like to make it. Or rather, they don't like to appear to like making money. When you want to pay an Englishman, especially for a service, he is invariably uncomfortable about it, looking sheepish and really sorry to bother you about something so embarrassing. Further, American-style salesmanship is unknown. On arriving in York, I tried to buy a used Nissan from a Citroen dealer near my apartment. The salesman was so low key that at the point in the conversation in which an American car salesman would be promising to name all his children and grandchildren after me, I had to prompt him about all the features of the car he was supposed to be telling me about. "Great fuel efficiency!" I offered. "If you like that sort of thing," he said. In light of the cost of the used car, I asked whether it might be a better idea to buy a new Citroen. "Oh, no," he replied. "You definitely would not want a Citroen."

In restaurants, it's nearly impossible to get the bill. For some reason, English restauranteurs imagine that diners want to linger long after their meal, and they don't like to spoil all that lingering with anything sordid like a bill. The friendly, attentive waiter who was ever so helpful during dinner is nowhere to be found afterward. You have to track him down hiding behind a pillar and thrust money into his pockets if you don't want to spend the entire evening waiting. We came up with the idea of bringing a pack of cards with us to restaurants. Playing cards often attracts the interest of the waiters, and if not, you at least get in a good game of pinochle waiting for the bill.

The English ambivalence about money extends to ambivalence about work. In every type of business involved with the public, English people are invariably polite and helpful, but more committed to putting in a good day's work than to advancing the success of their business. Unable to find Epsom salts in a pharmacy, I asked the friendly cashier whether they stocked them. He produced a box from behind the counter, and explained that because people kept coming in and buying Epsom salts, he hid them so they wouldn't run out!

In a London Starbucks with an English friend, we saw a very outgoing, solicitous barista. She seemed English to me, but my friend was deeply disturbed. She thought that no Englishwoman would ever be so customer-oriented. She finally couldn't take it anymore and asked the young woman where she was from. "New Zealand," she answered. My friend was deeply relieved; this enthusiastic young woman had upset her whole sense of what it means to be English.

The English discomfort about money extends to charitable giving. Like other Europeans, wealthy English people give far less to charity than comparable Americans do, as they expect the government to take care of things. However, when they do contribute, they do not want too much recognition. American universities or hospitals have the name of a donor on just about every building, room, or major piece of equipment. You'll see the Irving and Stella Katzenbaum Linen Supply Closet, for example. In contrast, major donors in England try to avoid trumpeting their donations. Buildings will usually contain a plaque indicating the distinguished (preferably royal) person who attended the opening, but not necessarily the person who made the donation of millions of pounds that made it possible.

BANKING

anks in England are like those in the United States except that, once again, they are a bit uncomfortable about the money part.

When I first arrived in England, I tried to open a savings account at a bank near my office in York. A very pleasant young woman explained to me that she was ever so very sorry, but I couldn't open an account because the bank didn't yet have a relationship with me. I was astonished. I had a stack of English money with a picture of the queen on every bill obtained with my American bankcard from this very own bank's ATM just outside the building where we were talking. The ATM, of course, did not know or care if I was an ax murderer, a member of the Taliban, or George W. Bush; it gaily and democratically handed out cash money to everyone. Yet inside the same bank, I had to have a special relationship to open an account! The nice young woman explained that I could get a letter from my employer introducing me to them and all would be well, but I had to have a bank account to rent an apartment I'd provisionally signed up for, it was Saturday morning, and it would take a while to get a letter. She was terribly sorry.

I considered going out and buying a gun and a ski mask, returning with my money in a paper sack, and saying, "Take this money and open an account, and no one gets hurt," but it's impossible in England to buy a gun, and not so easy to find a ski mask. Besides, where I come from, going into a bank wearing a ski mask but no gun is considered half-dressed, like wearing a tuxedo jacket but no pants. So I went away. The apartment fell through, but I eventually got a letter and the bank then happily started me in a checking account. However, when I suggested opening a savings account as well, the teller refused, suggesting that we wait awhile to see how the checking account went. Four years later, I'm still waiting.

Like most immigrants, I send money back to the home country to support layabout relatives (in my case, twenty-something children). This requires monthly trips to the foreign exchange department of a bank in the center of York.

Once again, I've learned that banking in England is all about relationships. If I'm lucky, I deal with an incredibly friendly, capable teller who zips through my paperwork because she knows me, in the sense that she's seen my wife and me walking around town. If I'm not so lucky, I get a deeply suspicious teller who wants to know my mother's maiden name, the date of our last expenditure, the capital of Burundi, the prime minister of the Maldives, the square root of 361, and so on.

So my VIP treatment by the first teller is due to the highly banking-relevant act of walking around town. York has a famous lunatic asylum and two universities. How does our familiar teller know we're not just out on a day pass from one of them? (As indeed we are.)

SHOPPING HOURS (CLOSED ENCOUNTERS)

Like most urban Americans, I live near several grocery stores that are open twenty-four hours every day. Almost every store is open until 9:00, and everything is open on Sunday.

In England, you won't be surprised to hear, nothing is open after 5:00 except pubs and restaurants, and very little is open on Sundays. At least this is true in York. Everyone is working from nine to five, so who the heck is shopping when the stores are actually open? The result is that everyone in York goes shopping in the historic downtown on Saturday. This produces a sort of holiday spirit every week, and the city adds to it with various food festivals, morris dancers, brass bands, and performers of all sorts. The streets, closed to traffic, are so thronged with happy people that if you fainted, it would take you ten minutes to hit the pavement and be trampled to death.

I tend to work late and rarely go home before 7:00, so my personal knowledge of most shops in York is limited to Saturdays. I've gotten used to this, I guess, but once again, it seems terribly unenterprising. Here I am, a customer with ready money, and no one will stay open late enough to take it from me. One exception is in coastal resorts where the Pound Lands (=Dollar Stores) and purveyors of tacky souvenirs are open late and on Sunday. Holidaymakers take a Dionysian pleasure in shopping at all hours in Scarborough or Blackpool or Brighton; don't the shops in York take the clue?

Napoleon famously dismissed England as a nation of shopkeepers. Obviously, he'd never been there. England may be a nation of shop *owners*, but if they were really keeping shop, they'd stay open a little later.

DRIVING

The most important thing for Americans to know about driving in England is don't do it. Keeping left is the least of it, although this takes practice. For a long time, when I rented a car with a standard transmission (far more common and cheaper in the UK), I'd invariably try to shift the door handle rather than remember to shift with my left hand.

The bigger problem is with the roads. The motorways (freeways) follow the lines laid out by the ancient Romans. They are straight, efficient, and boring, like the ancient Romans themselves. However, Anglo Saxons and Vikings laid out the secondary roads, and they drank a lot. They have a lot of roundabouts, or what I'd call terror-go-rounds. There's some rule about how to go around roundabouts, but my personal rule is to keep going around on the inside until there are no cars around at all. In crowded and confusing cases, this could mean seven or eight circuits, but better safe than sorry.

The worst of it is how narrow English roads are, and parking is allowed everywhere. As a result, even on a major two-way road through a town, there is really space for only one American. In some Harry-Potter-esque leger-de-car, two English drivers, even two huge busses, can pass each other on a road that an American would hesitate to drive on by himself. On a really skinny motorcycle.

In Cornwall, even fairly major thoroughfares are so narrow that bushes on both sides can scratch your car at the same time on roads linking towns of some size. Wales is even worse. If you encounter another car on a secondary rural road in Wales, one of you has to find a slightly wider spot and nestle into the hedgerow. It can take an entire harrowing afternoon to go ten miles.

Everything about automobiles is hugely expensive in England. The car itself is not the problem. Fuel is more than eight dollars a gallon. Taxes and insurance are shocking, and repairs are worse. Then there are speed cameras. I once got lost in Manchester one evening, and was photographed going thirty miles an hour in a twenty-five-mile per hour zone. Ultimately, the Manchester police sent me a form asking my nationality and income (!). Foolishly, I told them the truth. I can only imagine the partying at police headquarters. We caught a rich American! Let's take the poor bugger for all he's worth! My five mile per hour indiscretion ended up costing me the equivalent of six hundred dollars.

Even knowing better, I tried to get a UK driver's license. I called the license bureau and found that there was nowhere in York I could apply. Not to worry, I'd go to an office next time I was in London, where, I was assured, I could show my US passport as identification and get sorted right away.

The London office turned out to be in suburban Wimbledon, and the train broke down a few miles away. I walked to Wimbledon, waited in a long line, and found out that in order to apply for a license I had to send my passport to Swansea for a month or more. Traveling back and forth frequently to the United States, this was impossible.

We finally gave up. After buying a car when we first got to England, we eventually gave it away to a Canadian friend. She's never forgiven us.

THE 5:17 TO LILLIPUT

I n England, children play a game called "sardines," much like hide-and-seek, except that one child hides and all the others seek. When a seeker finds the hider, she gets in with her, and in a while, all the children squeeze into the same closet. Much giggling is involved.[6]

British trains are a lot like this, but without the giggling. They are frequent and efficient, but always crowded and incredibly small.

British train seats make you pine for airline seats. They were obviously made for Lilliputians. Especially small and flexible Lilliputians.

Fortunately, the English are used to playing sardines, and they are perfectly suited to maintaining a dignified distance from a seatmate who spends two hours physically closer than some married couples ever get.

The patience and good humor of train passengers are tested even more by a reservation system used on most trains. You can reserve a seat, but if you fail to do so, or if you take an earlier or later train than the one you reserved, you find that every seat is already reserved. However, about a quarter to half of the people don't show up. But which ones? The seatless proletariat picks seats at random, ready to be ejected by the rightful holder. This creates a polite but testy barn dance. The seatless avoid taking seats too early (greater chance of ejection) or too late (other seatless persons get them first). A rather icy do-si-do ensues when you choose wrong and the seat holder shows up, looks puzzled, compares his or her ticket to the seat number, and hems and haws until the poacher gets the idea. It all works, sort of, if you know the social rules. In the

---

6   The royal version of this game is called Privy Council.

United States, weapons might be brandished, but we'd never use such a silly system in the first place.

Trains are not infrequently canceled, due to signal problems in Stevenage, and then an entire train's worth of passengers, now all without reservations, is inflicted on the next (already fully reserved). This makes the reservation barn dance even more important, as the losers will stand in the drafty, noisy, uncomfortable Loser Landing between the cars for hours. I was once on such a train and the ticket taker came through. "Don't you want to see my ticket?" I asked from the sardine-game Loser Landing. She gestured at the packed seething mass of Englishmen. "Do you think I'm crazy?" she answered.

GETTING SORTED

T he English are always talking about "getting sorted," which means setting things right that are not currently right. But it's all talk. Getting things sorted in England can be a full-time occupation, if it can be done at all.

My wife and I rented a year-old apartment in the middle of York, built on the site of the ancient Roman civilian town. One appealing feature was a combination washing machine and dryer. Almost immediately, the dryer broke. Ever since then, for more than three years, we've been notifying, then threatening, then cajoling, then begging the landlord to fix the dryer, while we've been hanging wet clothes all over the place like refugees. The landlord's agent is invariably helpful and concerned, and promises to get someone over right away. This has never happened.

The same thing has happened with all sorts of sorting we've needed. Sometimes a pair of comical Yorkshiremen come to look at heaters or lights or toilets or whatever, but I think they are always the same people, actors disguised as Yorkshiremen, who put on different wigs and clothing to pretend to be repairmen (think Laurel and Hardy, but without the know-how). They fiddle around with gauges or controls, fix nothing, and go away with a suggestion that we contact someone else. "Someone else" takes another month or two to show up, and the pair of Yorkshiremen who finally come look suspiciously familiar. I wonder if the long delays are intended to make it harder for us to remember that the new repairmen are really the old ones in disguise.

The difficulty getting things repaired is surprising in light of the high unemployment rates in nearby cities. You'd think that a place like York, located so near to places like Doncaster, Hull, and Sunderland, with endemic unemployment, would be training plumbers and technicians like crazy. They make a very good living, and obviously, only have to work when they feel like it. Instead, Poles and other Eastern Europeans, who are competent, hardworking, and have families to support back in Gdansk, are increasingly filling technical positions. Or maybe people from Doncaster go to acting school to learn to *pretend* to be repairmen.

TALES OF THE CRYPTO-TOFFS

As everyone knows (because the Walt Disney Corporation constantly tells them), England is obsessed with social class. This may be true, but in my observation, it's even more obsessed with being obsessed about social class (got that)?

If an Englishman has a working-class dad, or grandfather, or ancestor of any kind, he's bound to work it into every conversation. "Nice day," you might say. "Nice enough," he might answer. "Did I mention that my dad was a millworker in Huddersfield?"

In North America, people may mention their immigrant forebears, as in "My great-grandfather came from Italy with twenty-seven cents in his pocket." Or "When my grandfather came to America from Greece, he owned only one shipping line." This is said in part with pride in how far the speaker has come up the economic ladder, and in part to contrast with today's immigrants who (the speaker believes) seem to want success given to them on a silver platter.

In England, however, the obligatory Dad-was-a-miner speech is not one-upmanship, but more one-downmanship. It says, "even though I wear a tie and look like a toff, I'm only one generation from the mines." It's a sort of statement of solidarity with the working class, which makes a person more likeable and trustworthy, I suppose.

The problem, however, is that talking about your working-class ancestors is one of the many subtle indicators of toffness. Real working-class people don't harp on their working-class backgrounds; just like Americans, they'd rather be taken for middle class.

Fortunately, Americans in England automatically live outside of the class system. Rich or poor, regardless of who their antecedents were, an American is just a puzzled onlooker to the class system. They are allowed to make the most terrible gaffes that, for an English person, could fatally brand someone as working class, or a toff pretending to be working class, or a member of the working class pretending to be middle class, or a toff pretending to be working class in just such a way as to let you know that he or she is really upper class, or whatever. I think one reason Americans are popular in England is that no matter how long they've lived there, they have no idea how the class game works, so an English person can feel safe with them. Americans don't know that it matters hugely how you brew your tea, or whether they put the milk or the tea in first, and so on, which the English notice about other English people instinctively. Americans can usually tell a BBC (=toff) accent from local dialects, but the finer gradations of language and behavior escape us. In fact, I think it's a good idea for Americans to preserve their ignorance in this arena.

LANGUAGE

Americans and British people alike cherish the differences between our dialects. Some of these differences are just spelling (e.g., honor/honour), some just usage (e.g., in the hospital/in hospital), and some are straightforward vocabulary (e.g., truck/lorry). However, some differences have serious comic potential. Americans are aware of the possibilities of "knocking up" (getting someone pregnant in the United States, visiting in the UK), and "knickers" (shorts in the US, panties in the UK), which are worn on the "bum," and the paid attendance at a performance can be referred to as "bums on seats."

"Nappies" are diapers in the UK, not a cute word for napkins, which may be "serviettes" in certain circumstances. It's more subtle differences that are most likely to cause misunderstandings. In the United States, "brilliant" means truly outstanding, exceedingly intelligent. In England, it means "pretty good," especially in its offhand version, "brill." "Chuffed" means really excited in England, and while it doesn't exist in the United States, it sounds angry. The opposite of "chuffed" is "gutted," which sounds more as it should. The English ask for a bill, never a check (or cheque) in a restaurant, and if you ask for a check, the waiter thinks you're asking him to pay you!

Some British usages are so lacking in American and so useful that they are creeping into my vocabulary even in the United States. One is remit, usually as in "not my remit." We'd say "not in my job description," an indication of a bad attitude. Just as the Inuit are supposed to have a lot of words for snow, you'd expect the English to have a lot of words for "not my remit," a concept of apparently greater importance in the UK, where it's virtually impossible to sack (fire) anyone.

"Like teaching your granny to suck eggs," means telling someone something they already know. "She's a waste of space" is the worst insult ever, and "I don't have time for him" is only slightly less so. "Knackered" means half-dead with exhaustion, from the term "knacker's yard," which means a place where dead animals were rendered, or today, an auto salvage yard. To "chivvy" means to round up or organize with difficulty, a bit like herding cats. A "damp squib" is a fizzle, literally a wet fuse.

Another wonderful Britishism is "going pear-shaped," similar to the American "going haywire," but with a more compelling image. A scientist is a "boffin" (with the connotation of "nerd"). Something genuine is "pukka," from the Hindi. Something exact is "spot on," and custom-made is "bespoke." When a business is meeting its costs, it's "washing its face." All these somehow seem more useful or fun than their US equivalents.

Americans think the English use a lot of words that, in my experience, they rarely use. I rarely hear "cheerio," never hear girls referred to as "birds," never hear about "keeping a stiff upper lip," never hear anything about "rot."

One expression English people use all the time is "cheers." It sort of means "thanks" or "good-bye," but it is used after "thank-yous" and "good-byes" have already been exchanged, and nothing more is really needed, when an American would have already finished a conversation and is heading off purposefully in a different direction. I've never met an American, no matter how long a resident in the UK, who uses "cheers" as the English do, because it just does not substitute for anything an American would say. The definition of "cheers" in a British-American dictionary should be " ".

There is a lot more variation in dialect within the UK than between American and BBC English. Scots, especially from Glasgow and Dundee, are just as incomprehensible to the English as to Americans. West Yorkshiremen can only be understood after a lot of practice. The problem is that each region has its own pronunciation of vowels, but over time, you can learn the rules and things start to make sense. For example, in Yorkshire, "mud" and all other short *u* words have the same sound of the first syllable in "pudding," while in the South, "mud" is pronounced as Americans say it and as God intended.

The English have a huge advantage over us in language. Because they watch so many American movies, they understand every American dialect, while a movie made in parts of the UK for the UK market would literally need subtitles if shown in the United States (which it wouldn't be, of course). In fact, movies made in some parts of the UK would need subtitles for Englishmen.

PANTOS

One wonderful aspect of English culture that Americans know nothing about is pantos (for pantomimes), a Christmas-season tradition throughout the country. A panto is a play or a musical composed of corny jokes, stock characters, and extensive and enthusiastic audience involvement. People go to pantos presented by the same troupe for years on end. One tradition is the reading of letters from audience members, which invariably start, "I've been coming to the (fill in name of town) panto for thirty years, and it gets better every time."

The star of every panto is "the dame," always a man in drag. There is always a villain. The audience always, in unison, tells the dame, "He's standing right behind you!" when the villain is sneaking up on him/her, and the whole audience is invited to do competitive singing and other silly forms of participation. Every child in England goes to a panto, but so do people of all ages with or without children. And every one of them, Tory, Lib Dem, and Labour alike, participates with gusto in the silly songs, diving for sweets thrown to the audience, and so on.

The panto experience illustrates three important aspects of the English character: continuity, communalism, and silliness. Pantos are great fun, but people go to them each year because they've always gone to them each year. Everyone goes, and everyone participates regardless of age or social class. And everyone is just as silly as can be. By being silly together, English people assert their sense of community. How can you feel separate from people who howl with laughter at the same puns, sight gags, and pratfalls you do, in the same theater at the same time, every single year?

DANCING SHEEP

In North Yorkshire stands the seventeenth-century home of George Calvert, the original Lord Baltimore. George was secretary to James I. Talk about a lucky guy. Most secretaries are lucky if they get a watch or coffee mug with the company logo on it. George got the Chesapeake Bay.

In any case, as a loyal Baltimorean, I thought I should visit George's house, but every time I've tried, it's closed. This is fine, because in Yorkshire, as in every part of England, there is so much to see and do that Plan B or C or D is also likely to be wonderful.

On one such journey, I saw a flyer for a sheep fair in Masham and went to check it out. It was terrific. There were sheep with four horns, sheep of unusual colors, sheep with fat tails, sheep-judging contests, and sheep dog trials, all in a lovely market town in a beautiful setting. But the best thing about the sheep fair was a sheep show in which a very funny sheep farmer from New Zealand showed off his dancing sheep.

The dancing sheep show was on a square off the main square, where every square inch was full of eager English people of all ages. It was sort of a sheep panto. The New Zealander stood for more than an hour and sheared a sheep, told stories about sheep, complained about wool prices, told corny jokes, invited audience participation, told more corny jokes, and so on. He had six sheep standing on boxes. Their names were on the boxes, and he kept promising that those sheep would dance, but first he would show us one or two things about sheep that we'd find amusing.

The central dynamic of this whole performance, of course, is that everyone in the audience knew that sheep can't dance. Chewing is more or less the most complex behavior they know. So what the audience was waiting for was not to see sheep dance, which is impossible, but to see how the New Zealander was going to keep his promise. Besides, the journey was more fun than the destination.

After an hour or so, the New Zealander could delay no more. He put on some disco music and showed the sheep a few spirited steps. They did nothing. Finally, he got out a feed bucket and waved it to the music in front of each sheep in turn. Sure enough, they moved their heads to follow the feed bucket, and if you gave them the benefit of the doubt, those sheep danced. Sort of. The audience loved it.

I think the dancing sheep show is meant to teach a deep lesson. The one I went away with, anyway, is that the best way to go through life is to believe that eventually, the sheep will dance. A realist would have walked away, but realists don't have much fun.

The good-natured English audience in Masham was happy to be taken in by the dancing sheep. Next year, and the year after, they'll come back and be taken in again. Maybe the New Zealander will come up with some new jokes or new tricks. And maybe the sheep will learn to dance.

ENGLAND AND THE UNITED KINGDOM

T he English are seriously conflicted about who they really are. The problem is that the other nations of the United Kingdom, especially Scotland and Wales, are loudly asserting themselves and exerting more local control. A bit like Canadians with respect to the United States, the Scots and Welsh define themselves by their non-Englishness, and they are working hard to bring back their Celtic languages and distinct cultures. You really do hear Welsh spoken in Wales, even among children, and Scotland and Wales really do have histories separate from that of England. However, all of the nationalism within the UK leaves the English as the vanilla in the choc-van-straw, the default option, rather than its own ethnicity. Only slowly have the English discovered that they have their own flag (the Cross of St. George, not the Union Jack), but it still galls them that there is far more celebration (i.e., drinking) in England on St. Patrick's Day than on St. George's Day.

Traveling in Wales, an American is always especially welcome for not being English. If you indicate that you are aware that England is merely another nation within the UK, and that "England" is not a synonym for "UK," and that Wales in *not* in England, you make friends for life.

The English try to be politically correct, they really do, but England is so big (relative to Scotland and Wales) and has dominated its much smaller neighbors for so long that the English are always slipping up and thinking of Wales and Scotland as regions of England that just happen to have their own national soccer teams.

Northern Ireland

T here's nothing funny about Northern Ireland.

The Sea

The relationship between the English and the sea is legendary but complex. The sea they experience is not friendly. It is often stormy and terrifically cold. Surfers in Whitby wear wet suits even in summer. Sea bathing became popular in the Victorian age, but it was always more medical treatment than pleasure. Cold saltwater was supposed to be good for you.

Britain has really ferocious tides. In my part of America, the mid-Atlantic, we have tides, but basically, the ocean and bays stay put. In the British Isles, in contrast, you can often stand on the shore at low tide and see little evidence that an ocean ever existed. When the tide comes in, it floods the empty seabed very quickly. Every year, there are stories of idiots who walk out on the dry seabed and are then drowned when the sea comes rushing back.

In Shakespeare, characters are always saying, "We sail on the tide." I always thought this was merely poetic, but seeing the British tide in action, I understand it differently. Especially in the days of sailing or rowing, the condition of the tide must have been essential. On an outgoing tide, you could float right out from London to the English Channel, and back up river when the tide comes in. The sense of "now or never," as in "seize the tide," becomes apparent. You cast off when the tide is right, not when you might prefer to go.

The sea carried the Celts and then the Anglo-Saxons and then the Vikings and then the Normans to England in the first place, and then on to America and the rest of the world. The sea is so fundamental to the English psyche that it has been determined that the blood of every

Englishman is 96 percent seawater.[7] "Rule Britannia" claims "Britannia rules the waves." Perhaps, but surely the waves rule Britannia, too.

---

7   Note to boffins: Yes, I'm aware that this is true of every human on earth. But it's truer of Englishmen.

CULTURAL IMPERIALISM

As Americans, our newspapers are constantly reporting about how upstart nations are kicking our commercial butts, or will do so in a few years. First, it was the Soviet Union, then Germany, then Japan, then China, and most recently, it's (editor: fill in the name of the country kicking our commercial butts at press time). So it's always a shock to travel abroad and find out what a huge influence America has on the world. We may not make cars or electronic equipment that the world wants, but by gosh, we sing a lot of catchy songs.

This is especially true in England, where the (relative) lack of a language barrier leaves the population unprotected from a cultural tsunami from the United States. Every English person must hear a thousand American songs a week. Popular American TV shows are watched as much in Wolverhampton as they are in Milwaukee. Movies are overwhelmingly American. Media for children is especially American-dominated. I met an English woman who described her three-year-old daughter, who ordinarily speaks with a proper English accent, except that when she plays with her (movie-themed) dolls, she speaks to them in American English. Kids watch *The Simpsons* and *SpongeBob SquarePants* and *South Park*, which no one even thinks to dub with English accents.

Of course, English, Scottish, and Irish rock musicians are also popular in the United States, but they are so much part of a common musical culture that I doubt many Americans know or care who is American and who is not.

The most corrosive medium, television, spreads its evil influence in only one direction, west to east. English shows play to small highbrow audiences on public television in the United States, but when British TV has an idea bad enough for mainstream American TV (think reality TV and *The Office*), Americans make their own version. Many English actors appear in Hollywood movies, of course, but truly English productions rarely appear. American-made Broadway shows occupy most of the theaters in London's West End.

The huge influence of US mass culture on England causes a bit of resentment and a rather vague feeling among the English that something should be done to preserve a distinctly English culture. From a cultural perspective, the English are worried that the UK is becoming a mere region of a vast US-UK-Canadian-Australian-New Zealand empire headquartered in Hollywood and New York. American media has substantially erased regional variations within the United States; only the American South still has much of its own accent and separate traditions, and these are eroding fast. Could the same happen to England? It's a terrible thing to imagine, but *SpongeBob* is taking over. As an American, I say to my English friends that I am terribly, terribly sorry. But thanks for buying my American book.

CANADIANS IN BRITAIN

Canadians in the UK are very, very happy people. The Welsh and the Scots feel solidarity with them, because they see a parallel between their resentment toward a large neighbor (that would be England) and Canada's (that would be us). The English feel a common resentment toward a much larger friend and ally (us again). Much as the British love Americans as individuals, they are terribly concerned about our power, wealth, and cultural influence, especially in light of how crazy our political system seems to them (think Tea Party, which has zero support anywhere in Europe).

So Canadians, to the British, have all the positive personal attributes of Americans without the unsettling ability to annihilate the world by accident. Do you remember when Ronald Reagan said as a joke into a microphone, "Launch the missiles?" This was not funny abroad (or at home for that matter).

People in the UK, on hearing a North American accent, often ask where you're from. If you say Canada, they're invariably excited about it. Americans are ten pence a dozen, but Canadians? They're special.

For their part, being in England is deeply satisfying to the Canadian soul. Anglophone Canadians have a serious identity problem. What is Canadian culture? It's defined in terms of not being American, yet in reality, Canadians far more resemble the particular Americans nearest to them than they do other Canadians. Someone from Vancouver or Victoria is more like someone from Seattle or Portland than someone from New Brunswick, who is more like someone from Maine than someone from Winnipeg, who is more like someone from Minneapolis than someone from Calgary, who is more like someone from Denver than ... I think you get the point. To deal with this identity problem, English-speaking Canadians emphasize their Britishness and like to think of themselves as half-Brits.

The result is that Canadians in the UK find subtle ways to make their identity known. They wear maple leaf emblems on sweaters, or small maple leaf jewelry, or maple leaf tattoos. In contrast, Americans in the UK never wear US flags or jewelry. If asked about their accents, Canadians quickly and emphatically identify themselves as Canadians. If an English person refers to a mixed group of Americans and Canadians as "Americans," the Canadian will invariably pipe up to say "*North Americans*," much like Welsh or Scots in a group who are collectively referred to as "English."

I once went to an evening of Canadian music in York. It consisted of an English singer with no obvious connection to Canada who showed a movie about Joni Mitchell and sang some of her songs and those of Neil Young and Leonard Cohen. To an American, the idea of "Canadian" music is like "New Jersey" music; sure, there are musicians from New Jersey, but is there a distinctive New Jersey musical heritage? Every one of the influences mentioned by Joni Mitchell was an American, and every concert and broadcast shown took place in the United States. I doubt that there would be an "evening of Canadian music" in the United States (or even, perhaps, in Canada). There would certainly never be an "evening of American music" in the UK, since every evening is inescapably an evening of American music if a radio is on. Yet there was an English singer cashing in on the affection of the English for all things Canadian, and hoping (perhaps) to attract a few actual Canadians curious to find out what "Canadian music" is.

In the United States, Americans rarely think about Canadians at all, so it's curious to see how important it is to be Canadian in the UK. I think the experience of Canadians in the UK holds up a mirror to American experience. Throughout the world, people think a lot about Americans, for better or (usually) worse, because America is uniquely able to do good or harm anywhere, usually without even intending to. Every individual American personifies the hopes and fears about our country felt by the people we encounter abroad. Canadians are free of all this. Other than harp seals, no one in the world sits up at night worrying about what Canada might do or fail to do.

I often suspect that some of the people I see in England sporting the most obvious maple leaves may be from Wisconsin or Pennsylvania. In fact, during the final years of the Bush administration, I'm sure that a large percentage of Americans in Britain were pretending to be Canadians. The day Obama was elected, there was a definite smell in the air of burning maple leaves, as Americans were finally free to cast aside their disguises.

For French-Canadians, of course, none of the above applies. They don't come to England in the first place. They've already had it up to here with *les têtes carrés*, and don't need to go looking for them elsewhere. Instead, when they travel, they go to the one place where they know their language and culture and colorful bilingual money with beavers on it will be familiar and appreciated: Florida.

THE EUROPEAN UNION?

Long, long ago, when I was in college, a bicycle dealer in Portland, Oregon, offered a discount on a Japanese bicycle based on the number of bottle caps you brought into his store. I got the man who filled our dormitory Coke machine to give me all his bottle caps (note to young people: bottles used to have caps that you pried off and left in the machine). Using this strategy, I got this bicycle for next to nothing.

Bottle-cap discounts pretty much exhausts my knowledge of economics, so perhaps the European Union is a really good idea for the UK. From a political perspective, maybe it engages Germans and Frenchmen in petty squabbles in the European Parliament that divert them from the kinds of competition that used to cause a whole lot of trouble. For Englishmen, the EU solves the problem of what to do with all those worthless Belgian francs left over at the end of your trip.

But as an American, England being in the EU sucks. Who's your buddy? Who's your pal? Remember Roosevelt? Eisenhower? Lend-Lease? John F. Kennedy? Reagan at the Berlin Wall? Jimmy Carter? (Okay, you can forget about Jimmy Carter.) But now, when Americans arrive at Heathrow, all the Romanians and Latvians and Slovaks get in the fast lane, 'cause they're your new best mates, and Americans and Canadians, who rescued your butts on many an occasion, line up in the slow lane with the people from Togo and Fiji.

Everywhere you go in England, you'll hear American and Canadian accents, not to mention US culture and products. Yet outside of London, you hardly ever hear French or German spoken. You do hear a lot of Polish, but as soon as these people save up enough money, they are headed back to Krakow (the UK can no longer get by without them, but that's another story).

Every summer, at beach resorts and swimming pools throughout the eastern United States, tens of thousands of young Russians arrive to work. Russians! The same people who used to make us crawl under our desks at school for nuclear attack drills! They're lovely, by the way, and ever so sorry for the Cold War, which they were too young to have had a hand in. But still, why Russians instead of nice British or French or Italian or Polish young people? Because Russians, like Americans, Canadians, and Fijians, are not part of the EU, and the young people who are part of the EU get to work in English beach resorts like Skegness, which is just as bad as it sounds.

Any third-grader can see that this whole EU business makes no sense, and is bound to come to smash. You can't indoctrinate your kids with *SpongeBob* and *The Simpsons* and *Friends* and consistently fail to teach them any foreign language whatever, and then tell them that they've been friended on Facebook by Bulgarians but Americans are off limits. It's just not possible.

So here's my proposal. The UK can keep its EU membership, if that's good for supporting sugar beet prices or limiting sugar beet prices or whatever the UK wants sugar beet prices to do. However, the UK, United States, Canada, Australia, New Zealand, and maybe a few other countries[8] should form a *cultural* union, which has the following rules:

1. Everyone has to speak English, and no more than 2 percent of the population is allowed to speak any other language well enough to order at McDonald's without pointing.

2. Everyone has to watch at least two hours of American television every day. One American movie per week may be substituted.

---

8   Like Ireland. I don't think Ireland would want to join, but they'd be welcome if they did.

3. There will be no import duties among cultural union members on decent music, movies, and books. There will be a 100 percent tax on ABBA CDs.

4. At each member country's border, citizens of a cultural union country get to go in a really fast lane if they can sing "Crocodile Rock" by Elton John, or a comparable song of uncertain but definitely US/UK/Canadian/Australian origin.

GOVERNMENT

England and the United States have completely different ideas about government. In the United States, government is expected to be incompetent, annoying, and corrupt, and the only reason we tolerate it is that it can be highly amusing. We elect earnest former student council presidents so they'll go away to Washington instead of boring us with their latest plans for arbitration reform, whatever that is. We do not count on government for anything except national defense, and even there we keep an awful lot of guns, just in case.

The UK has a House of Lords to fulfill the main function of the US Congress (i.e., getting into hilarious scandals and saying demented things), but they don't actually let the House of Lords run anything. They're like children in the backseat with a toy steering wheel not actually connected to anything, except that they are in fact distinguished-looking barons and duchesses muttering angrily about the Socialists banning foxhunting. Basically, the House of Commons gets to pass the laws and run the country, and the House of Lords gets to say, "Harrumph." However, the rest of the government is rather serious, and people actually count on it to do things.

One scary aspect of this was illustrated in the great blizzard of 2009–2010. In York, anyway, there were snowplows for the roads, but no one ever shoveled the sidewalks. Why? I learned that some people apparently thought it was *illegal* to shovel their own sidewalks, because they are government property. Right in the commercial heart of York, snow lay for weeks and became ice and slush. The one exception: a Chinese grocery, whose staff quite sensibly did not trust the government to do anything, as it demonstrably was not doing. Everyone else patiently waited for the government to get things sorted. I think they would have waited until Hull froze over.

The National Health Service is a marvel of government efficiency. Since 1948, it has provided free healthcare to British citizens and visitors alike. Because of the NHS, however, the British government has a real, financial interest in your health and well-being. When anyone in the UK, rich or poor, has a baby, the NHS sends out a nurse to periodically visit mother and baby at home, until the mother forcibly ejects the nurse or the baby starts shaving, whichever comes first. To an American, this is astonishing and a little worrisome. A bit of advice for young mothers is appreciated, of course, but there is a subtle message that this is not entirely your baby, ma'am, it is also a future contributing member of British society, so I hope you're taking good care of our common property, little Alistair here, or as we like to call him, Case #37QZ197-H.

Because the British government is actually expected to do things, the UK elects people believed to be competent, not just amusingly inept. For example, the British prime minister has to participate frequently in "question time," in which he or she must respond *on television* to questions from hostile members of Parliament. This takes broad knowledge, great skill, and a good sense of humor (or humour, in this case). Imagine, for a moment, George W. Bush doing question time and you'll understand how extraordinary this is. A UK political party would never put up a person like George W. Bush for prime minister, because he'd be eaten alive by question time (on the other hand, Bill Clinton would have loved it).

Another great thing about UK government is that they have Liberal Democrats, or Lib Dems, a middle-of-the-road third party. Lib Dems are intelligent, honest, earnest-to-a-fault, and good-government types, which is why their electoral possibilities are nil. It's as though a bunch of Canadians somehow got elected to the US Congress. Jimmy Carter would probably be a Lib Dem if he were British. In the national elections of 2010, the Lib Dem leader, Nick Clegg, was deemed to have won debates with Gordon Brown and David Cameron hands down, but the Lib Dems still did not get more votes than usual. They did get to be part of a coalition with the Conservatives, but within three weeks, everyone forgot about them. A great thing about Lib Dems for an American in England is that in discussions about politics, mentioning them is inherently funny, much in the way it used to be instantly funny to mention the hapless Chicago Cubs. So you can sound sort of "in the know" without knowing anything at all.

As the Sun Sets ...

And so we leave the emerald-green shores of the lovely island of Britain with its friendly natives, exotic customs, and ancient traditions. A land that looks strangely like ours with a vaguely familiar language, but, charmingly, one we will never really comprehend. I hope this little book makes some small contribution to misunderstanding between our great nations.